Blastoff! Readers are carefully developed by literacy experts to build reading stamina and move students toward fluency by combining standards-based content with developmentally appropriate text.

LEVELS

Level 1 provides the most support through repetition of high-frequency words, light text, predictable sentence patterns, and strong visual support.

Level 2 offers early readers a bit more challenge through varied sentences, increased text load, and text-supportive special features.

Level 3 advances early-fluent readers toward fluency through increased text load, less reliance on photos, advancing concepts, longer sentences, and more complex special features.

★ **Blastoff! Universe**

Reading Level

Grade K → Grades 1–3 → Grade 4

This edition first published in 2024 by Bellwether Media, Inc.

No part of this publication may be reproduced in whole or in part without written permission of the publisher. For information regarding permission, write to Bellwether Media, Inc., Attention: Permissions Department, 6012 Blue Circle Drive, Minnetonka, MN 55343.

Library of Congress Cataloging-in-Publication Data

Names: Davies, Monika, author.
Title: Ukraine / by Monika Davies.
Description: Minneapolis, MN : Bellwether Media, Inc., 2024. | Series: Blastoff! Readers : countries of the world | Includes bibliographical references and index. | Audience: Ages 5-8 | Audience: Grades 2-3 | Summary: "Relevant images match informative text in this introduction to Ukraine. Intended for students in kindergarten through third grade"– Provided by publisher.
Identifiers: LCCN 2023003566 (print) | LCCN 2023003567 (ebook) | ISBN 9798886874358 (library binding) | ISBN 9798886876239 (ebook)
Subjects: LCSH: Ukraine–Juvenile literature.
Classification: LCC DK508.515 .D38 2024 (print) | LCC DK508.515 (ebook) | DDC 947.7–dc23/eng/20230127
LC record available at https://lccn.loc.gov/2023003566
LC ebook record available at https://lccn.loc.gov/2023003567

Text copyright © 2024 by Bellwether Media, Inc. BLASTOFF! READERS and associated logos are trademarks and/or registered trademarks of Bellwether Media, Inc.

Editor: Rebecca Sabelko   Designer: Gabriel Hilger

Printed in the United States of America, North Mankato, MN.

Table of Contents

All About Ukraine	4
Land and Animals	6
Life in Ukraine	12
Ukraine Facts	20
Glossary	22
To Learn More	23
Index	24

All About Ukraine

Kyiv

Ukraine is in eastern Europe. It is Europe's second-largest country! Its capital is Kyiv.

Many crops grow in Ukraine. Grain and sunflower fields spread far and wide.

Land and Animals

Flat **steppes** cover much of Ukraine. Thousands of rivers flow through the country.

Marshes are found in the north. Mountains stand tall in the west and south.

marsh

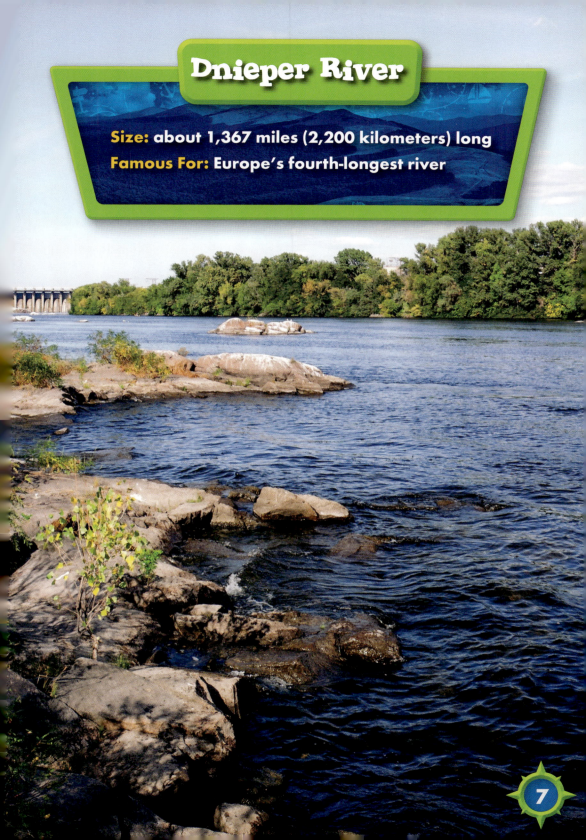

Dnieper River

Size: about 1,367 miles (2,200 kilometers) long
Famous For: Europe's fourth-longest river

Most of Ukraine has cold winters. Summers are warm. Most rain falls in June and July.

The weather is warm and mild in the south.

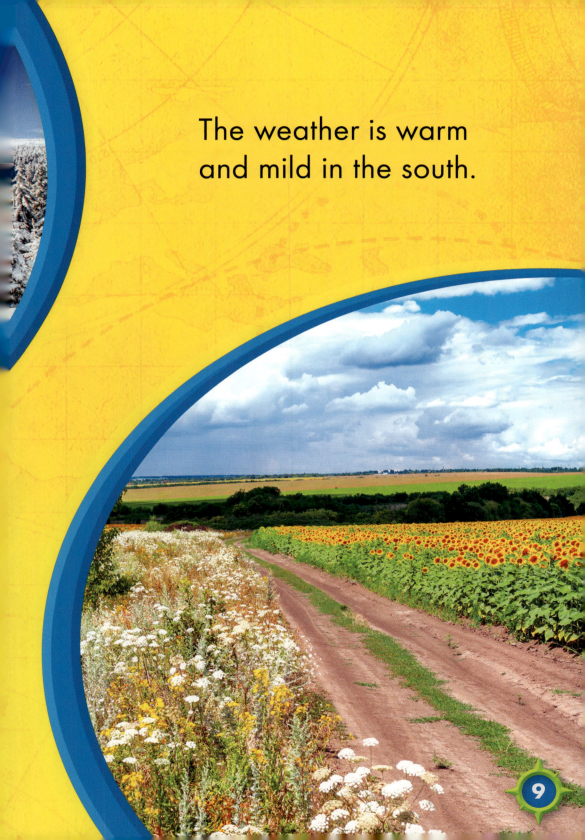

Wolves **prowl** in the steppes and mountains. Polecats hunt ground squirrels.

wood grouse

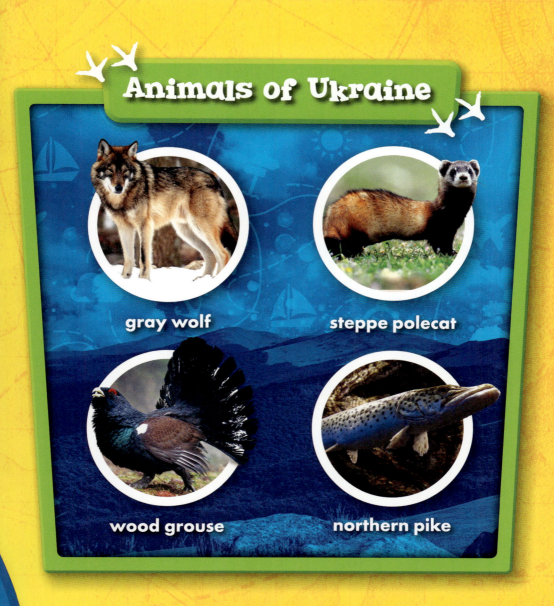

Animals of Ukraine

gray wolf

steppe polecat

wood grouse

northern pike

Grouse fly overhead. Over 200 kinds of fish swim in the rivers!

Life in Ukraine

Many Ukrainians are **Orthodox Christians**. Ukrainian is the country's main language.

People often live in cities or towns. Kyiv is the largest city.

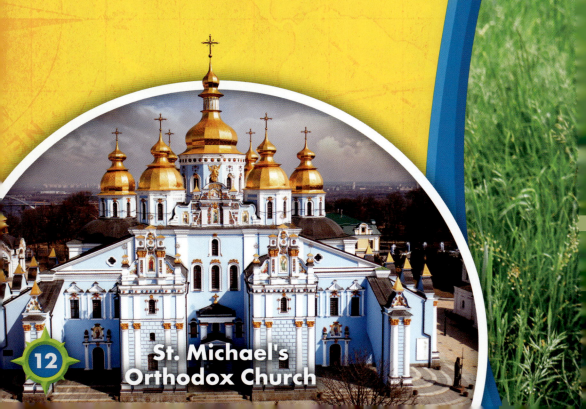

St. Michael's Orthodox Church

folk music

Folk art is a key part of Ukrainian **culture**. People enjoy **traditional** folk music.

Soccer is a top sport. Many people also play volleyball or go swimming.

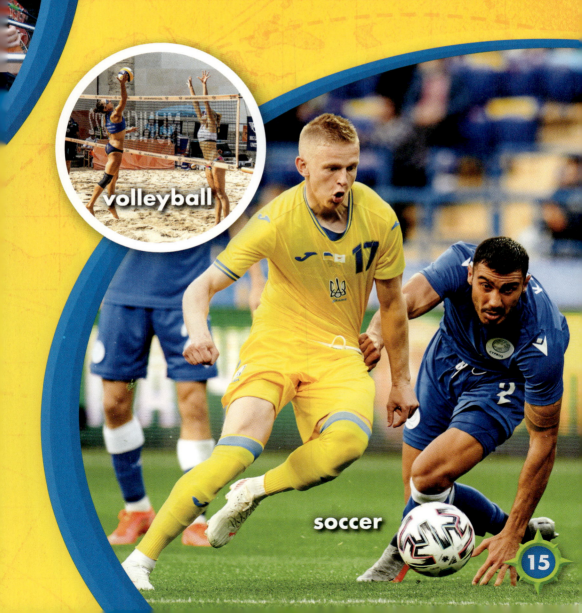

Ukrainians have many favorite dishes. *Borscht* is a beet soup served hot or cold. *Varenyky* are stuffed dumplings.

Ukrainian Foods

borscht

varenyky

holubtsi

verguny

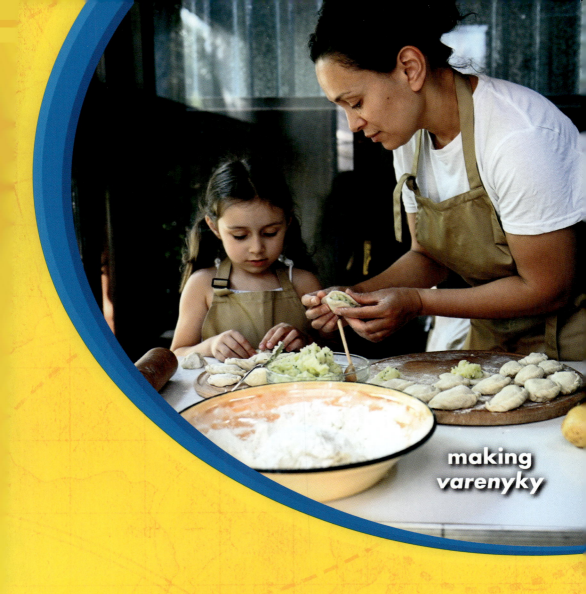

making varenyky

Holubtsi are cabbage rolls. People enjoy sweet treats called *verguny*.

Christians **celebrate** Easter. They make painted eggs called *pysanky*.

Independence Day

August 24 is Independence Day. People wave flags and light fireworks. This national holiday is important to Ukrainians!

Ukraine Facts

Size:
233,032 square miles
(603,550 square kilometers)

Population:
43,528,136 (2022)

National Holiday:
Independence Day (August 24)

Main Language:
Ukrainian

Capital City:
Kyiv

Famous Face

Name: Volodymyr Zelensky

Famous For: sixth president of Ukraine

Religions

Ukrainian Orthodox: 80%

other: 10% Ukrainian Catholic: 10%

Top Landmarks

Potemkin Stairs

Probiy Waterfall

St. Sophia Cathedral

Glossary

celebrate—to do something special or fun for an event, occasion, or holiday

culture—customs and beliefs of a certain group of people

marshes—areas of wet land that have many types of plants

Orthodox Christians—people who follow Christianity in the same way it was first followed; Christians are people who believe in the words of Jesus Christ.

prowl—to move quietly while on the hunt

steppes—dry, flat lands in areas with wide temperature ranges

traditional—related to customs, ideas, or beliefs handed down from one generation to the next

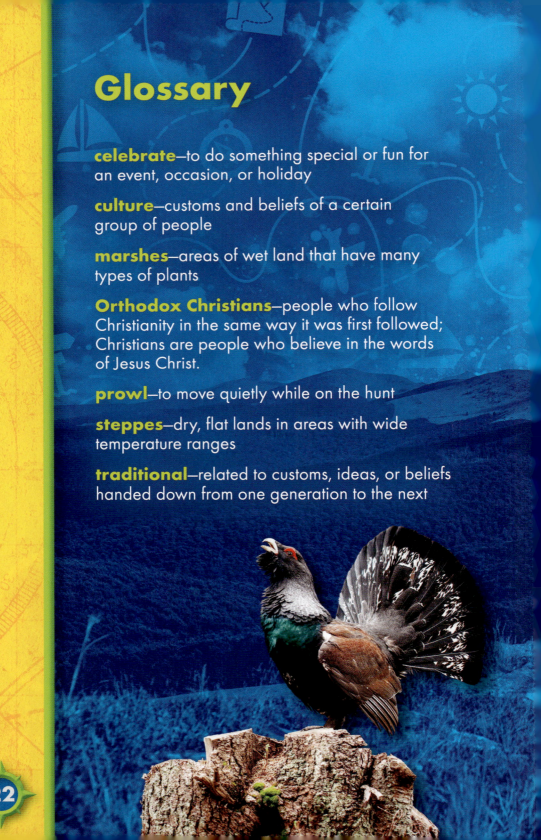

To Learn More

AT THE LIBRARY
Adamson, Thomas K. *Soccer*. Minneapolis, Minn.: Bellwether Media, 2020.

Dean, Sonny. *We Stand with Ukraine*. Bangor, Maine: Little Lambda Books, 2022.

Spanier, Kristine. *Ukraine*. Minneapolis, Minn.: Jump!, 2023.

ON THE WEB

Factsurfer.com gives you a safe, fun way to find more information.

1. Go to www.factsurfer.com.
2. Enter "Ukraine" into the search box and click 🔍.
3. Select your book cover to see a list of related content.

Index

animals, 10, 11
capital (see Kyiv)
cities, 12
crops, 5
Dnieper River, 7
Easter, 18
Europe, 4
folk art, 14
folk music, 14
food, 16, 17
Independence Day, 19
Kyiv, 4, 5, 12
map, 5
marshes, 6
mountains, 6, 10
Orthodox Christians, 12, 18
people, 12, 14, 15, 17, 19

pysanky, 18
rain, 8
rivers, 6, 7, 11
say hello, 13
soccer, 15
steppes, 6, 10
summer, 8
swimming, 15
Ukraine facts, 20–21
Ukrainian, 12, 13
volleyball, 15
weather, 9
winter, 8

The images in this book are reproduced through the courtesy of: Phant, front cover, p. 21 (St. Sophia Cathedral); Creative Travel Projects, front cover; Symon Bartos, pp. 2-3; Labrador Photo Video, p. 3; Ingus Kruklitis, pp. 4-5; Ganna Zelinska, p. 6; saha_stozhko, pp. 6-7; Standret, pp. 8-9; Yurikr, p. 9; eternal_aviv, p. 10; bpm82, p. 11 (gray wolf); altair, p. 11 (steppe polecat); Josef Cink, p. 11 (wood grouse); Anney_Lier, p. 11 (northern pike); Ruslan Lytvyn, p. 12; Oleh_Slobodeniuk, pp. 12-13; deniska_ua, pp. 14-15; Rudolf Ernst, p. 15 (volleyball); Vitalii Vitleo, p. 15 (soccer); Sokor Space, p. 16 (*borscht*); Smile Studio, p. 16 (*varenyky*); RomanaMart, p. 16 (*holubtsi*); zoryanchik, p. 16 (*verguny*); Tara Grebinets, p. 17; Zysko Sergii, pp. 18-19; titoOnz, p. 20 (flag); Alexandros Michailidis, p. 20 (Volodymyr Zelensky); Sergii Figurnyi, p. 21 (Potemkin Stairs); Nataliia Dvukhimenna, p. 21 (Probiy Waterfall); Matej Ziak, pp. 22-23.